Mushrooms and toadst[illegible]
fungus. Some are edible, but some are
poisonous. It is very difficult to tell them
apart.

Mushrooms and toadstools have a stem that comes up from the ground with a cap on top. Under the cap, there are lines running out from the middle. These lines are called gills.

On the gills are spores. Spores are the seeds of mushrooms and toadstools. There are thousands of spores on the gills of a mushroom.

The spores travel on the wind. When they land, they develop small white threads. Mushrooms or toadstools develop from these threads.

Mushrooms and toadstools do not have roots. Instead the small white threads spread out from the stem under the ground. The stem is made up of these threads.

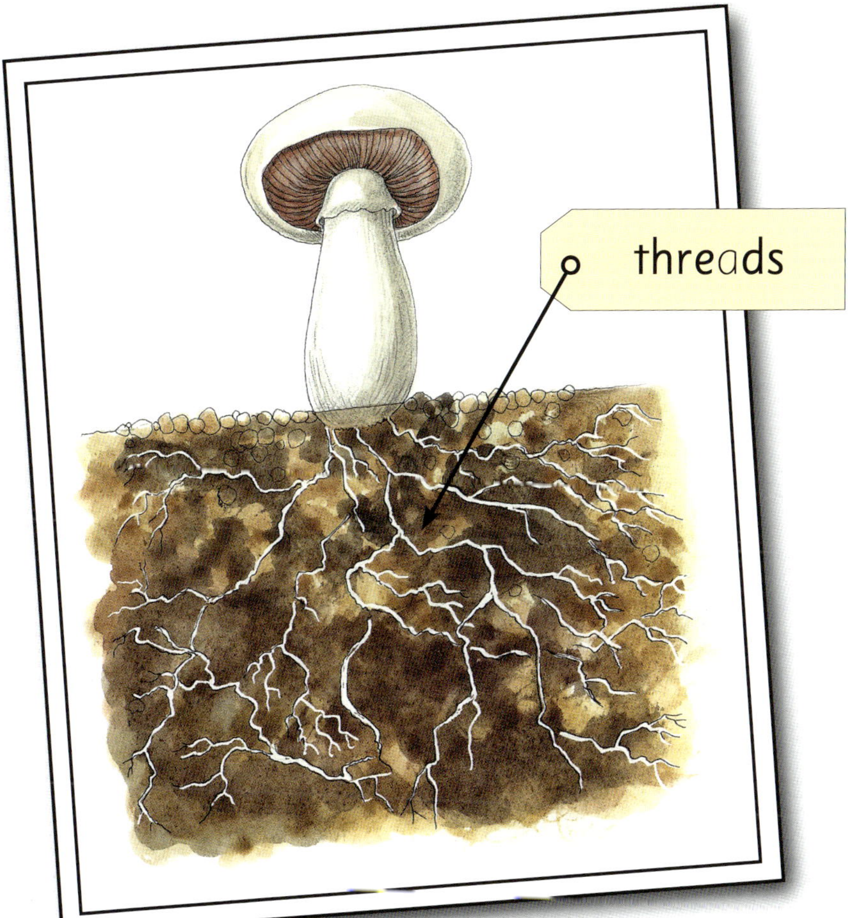

Mushrooms are often found in rings. The threads under the ground travel out and so the ring gets a bit bigger. The threads and mushrooms in the middle of the ring die.

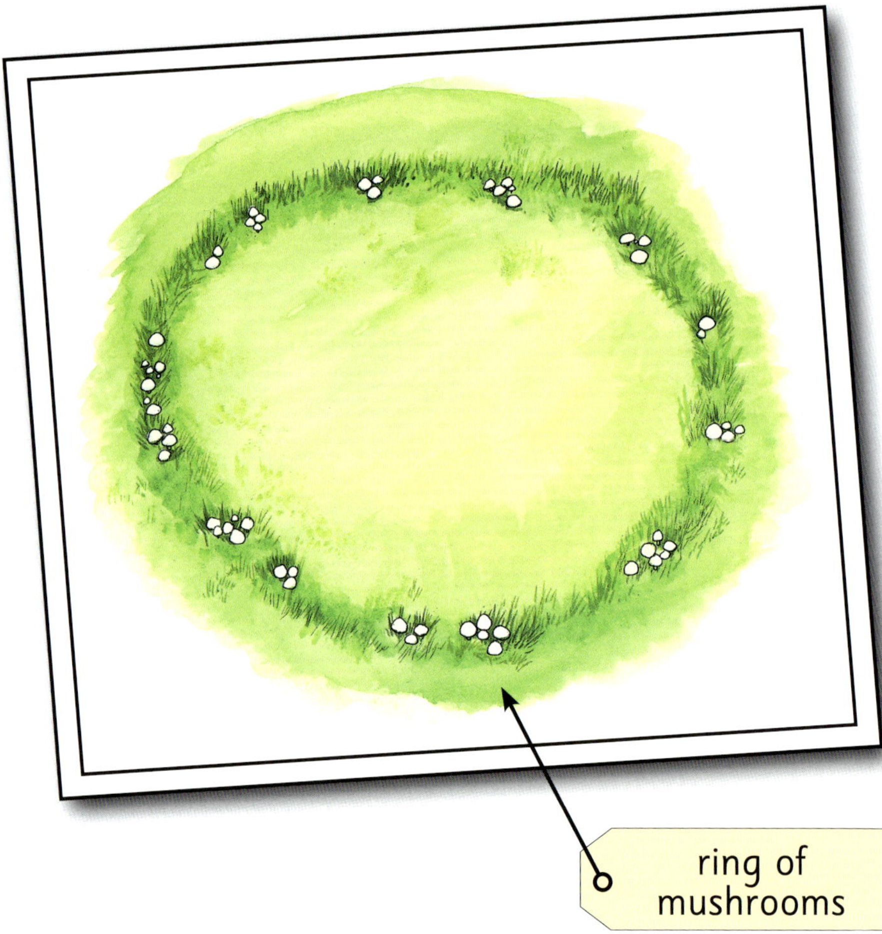

Mushrooms and toadstools start out looking like small buttons. The gills under the cap cannot be seen as the skin on the top is attached to the stem. As the mushroom or toadstool gets bigger, the skin stretches until it rips. You can see the ring of skin on the stem where it was attached.

Mushrooms and toadstools use the threads under the ground to get food. A liquid seeps out of the threads and into the soil, or wood, where the mushroom is. This liquid makes the dead stuff in the soil, or wood, liquid too. The threads then take in all this liquid as food, and it travels up the stem to the rest of the mushroom or toadstool.

Mushrooms and toadstools are found in woods, on trees, in dark damp spots, as well as in gardens.

The deathcap toadstool is very poisonous. It has a little cup at the bottom of the stem. It starts with a pointed white cap, but as it gets bigger, the cap gets flatter and darker. It has a sweet, sickly smell.

Bracket fungus is found on trees. It rots the wood of the tree. Bracket fungus can get very big. Some live on dead wood, but some attack living trees.

These mushrooms are shaggy inkcaps. The cap twists up and a dark liquid drips to the ground. They are often seen on the side of roads or on rubbish dumps.

Puffballs are round, white mushrooms. They can get as big as footballs. When they are ripe, they explode and a cloud of spores puffs out.

This is a stinkhorn. It starts as a small, white ball. When it gets bigger, it has a dark cap. The cap is very smelly. This smell attracts flies.

The fungus called dead man's fingers is found on tree stumps. It is black on the outside but white on the inside. It has a short, twisted stem which gets bigger at the top so they look a bit like fingers, which is where it gets its name from.

Truffles are a sort of fungus that develop under the ground. Truffles are used in cooking and are very expensive. Pigs can smell truffles. Farmers train pigs to root out the truffles.